Body Books

Eating

Anna Sandeman
Illustrated by Ian Thompson

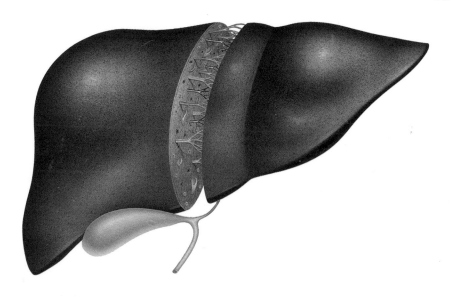

COPPER BEECH BOOKS

BROOKFIELD, CONNECTICUT

Copyright © 1995 Aladdin Books Ltd.
Produced by Aladdin Books Limited
28 Percy Street
London W1P 0LD

Designed by David West
 Children's Book Design
 Designer: Edward Simkins
 Editor: Liz White
 Picture Research: Brooks Krikler
 Research
 Consultants: Dr. R. Levene, M.D.
Jan Bastoncino, Dip. Ed.

First published in Great Britain in
1995 by Watts Books, London

First published in 1995
in the United States by Copper Beech Books,
an imprint of The Millbrook Press
2 Old New Milford Road
Brookfield, Connecticut 06804

Printed in Belgium

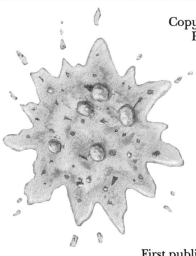

**Library of Congress Cataloging-
in-Publication Data**
Sandeman, Anna.
Eating / by Anna Sandeman;
illustrated by Ian Thompson.
p. cm.–(Body books)
Includes index.
ISBN 1-56294-945-4 (lib. bdg.)
1. Digestion–Juvenile literature. 2.
Gastrointestinal system–Juvenile
literature. [1. Digestive system.] I.
Thompson, Ian, 1964- ill. II. Title. III.
Series: Sandeman, Anna. Body books.
QP145.S26 1995
612.3–dc20   95-14022   CIP   AC

Photocredits
Abbreviations: t-top, m-middle, b-bottom, r-right, l-left
All the photos in this book are by Roger Vlitos except:
6t, 7t, 8-9b, 13b, 23tr, 23mr & 28-29t Frank Spooner
Pictures; 22r & 23br Paul Nightingale; 23l Eye
Ubiquitous; 28m Associated British Pictures Co.
(Courtesy Kobal Collection)

Contents

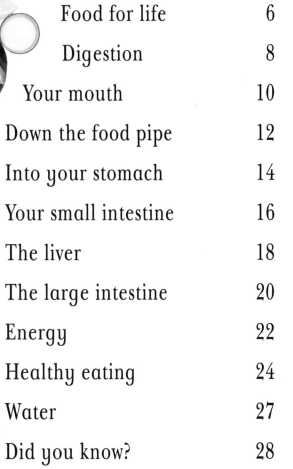

Food for life

All animals must eat to stay alive. Food is needed for energy and growth. Food also helps to mend parts of the body which have been hurt.

The kind of food each animal eats depends on where it lives, its size, shape, and strength. Monkeys will eat almost anything they can find. Penguins dive for fish in the icy Antarctic sea. They swallow a fish in a single gulp. Lions chase zebras across the hot African plains. They use sharp teeth to chew meat off the bone.

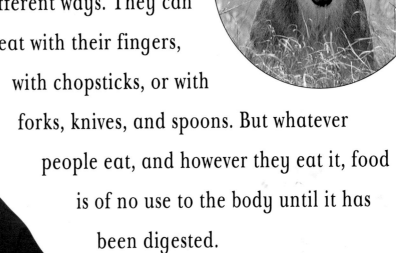

People live all over the world. They eat a wide variety of foods, prepared and cooked in many different ways. They can eat with their fingers, with chopsticks, or with forks, knives, and spoons. But whatever people eat, and however they eat it, food is of no use to the body until it has been digested.

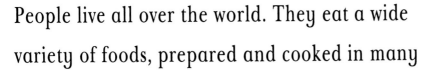

Digestion

Digestion starts as soon as you put food in your mouth. It carries on for about 20 hours as the food travels through your digestive system. This is a series of tunnels and caves inside your body. These are all different sizes, shapes, and lengths.

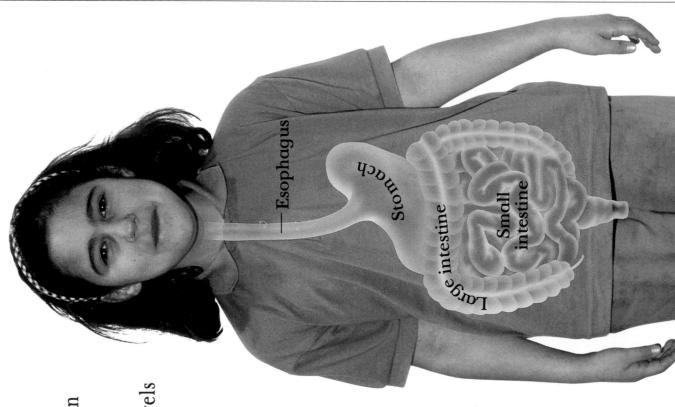

Esophagus

Stomach

Large intestine

Small intestine

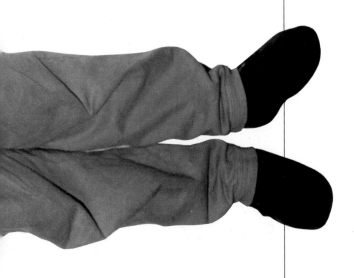

If they were laid in a straight line, they would stretch more than 26 feet (eight meters) – the average width of a swimming pool!

Your body digests food slowly by breaking it down into smaller pieces, separating it into useful parts – nutrients and waste matter. Food is completely digested when it has passed from your digestive system into your blood. Your blood then carries the nutrients around your body.

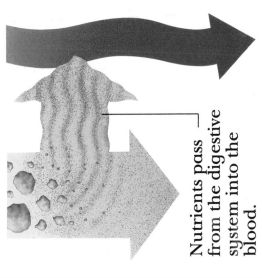

Food is broken down in the digestive system.

Nutrients pass from the digestive system into the blood.

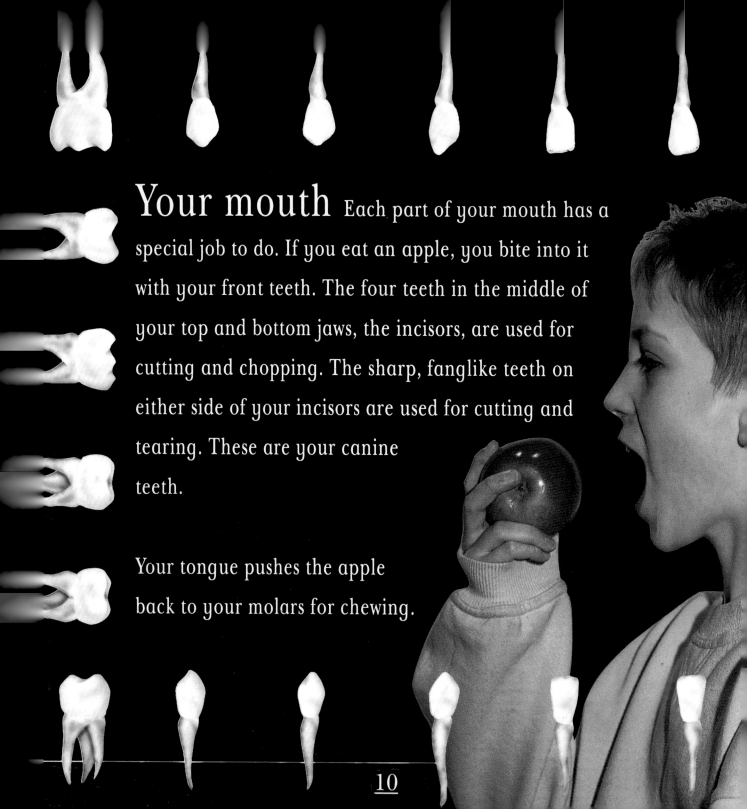

Your mouth

Each part of your mouth has a special job to do. If you eat an apple, you bite into it with your front teeth. The four teeth in the middle of your top and bottom jaws, the incisors, are used for cutting and chopping. The sharp, fanglike teeth on either side of your incisors are used for cutting and tearing. These are your canine teeth.

Your tongue pushes the apple back to your molars for chewing.

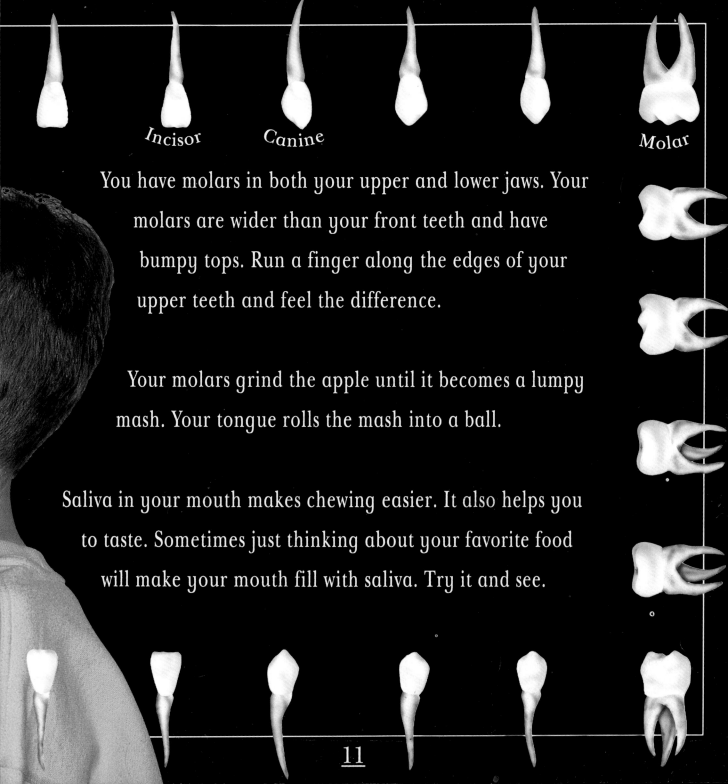

Incisor Canine Molar

You have molars in both your upper and lower jaws. Your molars are wider than your front teeth and have bumpy tops. Run a finger along the edges of your upper teeth and feel the difference.

Your molars grind the apple until it becomes a lumpy mash. Your tongue rolls the mash into a ball.

Saliva in your mouth makes chewing easier. It also helps you to taste. Sometimes just thinking about your favorite food will make your mouth fill with saliva. Try it and see.

Down the food pipe
Your tongue pushes the ball of mash into your food pipe. This is called your esophagus. As you swallow, a flap (your epiglottis) drops over your windpipe. This stops food from going down the wrong way.

Sometimes your epiglottis does not drop down in time. When this happens, you have to cough hard until the food is blown out of your windpipe.

Esophagus

Food mash

Your esophagus is a stretchy tube about ten inches (25 centimeters) long. Its walls are made of muscles which squeeze food downward. They do this without you thinking about it. To see how they work, put a tennis ball down a long sock. Like the muscles in your esophagus, you have to squeeze your hands hard together just behind the ball to move it along.

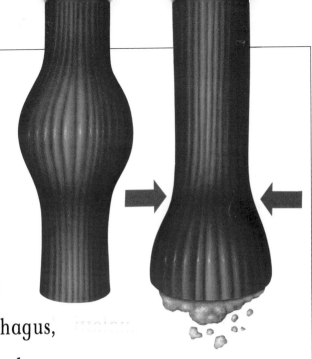

Muscles squeeze behind the food to push it down.

Because food is squeezed along your esophagus, and does not simply fall down it, it is possible to eat in almost any position – even standing on your head! This means that astronauts can enjoy a meal even when floating around their cabin! (But remember, it is safest to eat when you are upright.)

Into your stomach

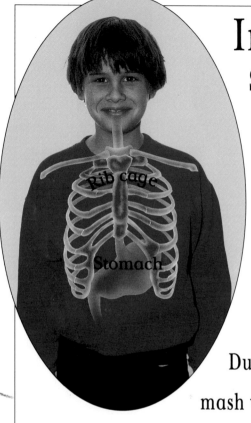

Rib cage

Stomach

At the bottom of your esophagus, the mash passes into your stomach. This is a stretchy bag shaped like a boxing glove. It lies just below your ribs. Food stays here for three to five hours.

During this time, your stomach churns the mash with gastric juices from your stomach wall. These juices kill any germs in the mash and help to break the food down into smaller parts. When the mash has turned into a kind of thick soup, it is ready to leave your stomach.

Gate of muscle

Food soup

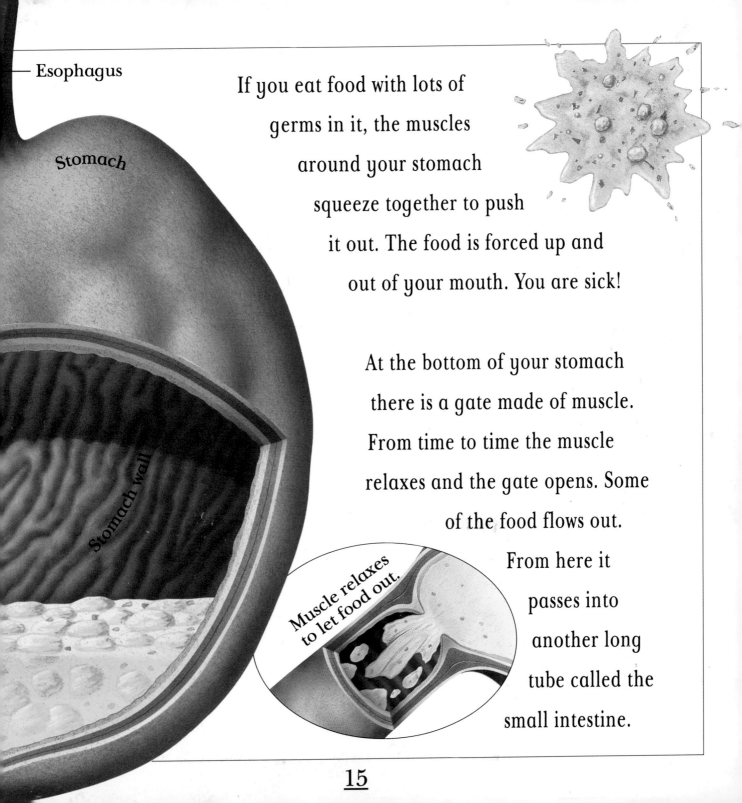

Esophagus

Stomach

Stomach wall

Muscle relaxes to let food out.

If you eat food with lots of germs in it, the muscles around your stomach squeeze together to push it out. The food is forced up and out of your mouth. You are sick!

At the bottom of your stomach there is a gate made of muscle. From time to time the muscle relaxes and the gate opens. Some of the food flows out. From here it passes into another long tube called the small intestine.

15

Your small intestine
Your small intestine is about 23 feet (seven meters) long. That's as long as five seven-year-olds laid head to toe! It can take up to four hours for the food to travel from one end to the other.

In the first part of the small intestine, food is mixed with juices from your pancreas and bile from your liver which help to break it down even further.

Liver

Pancreas

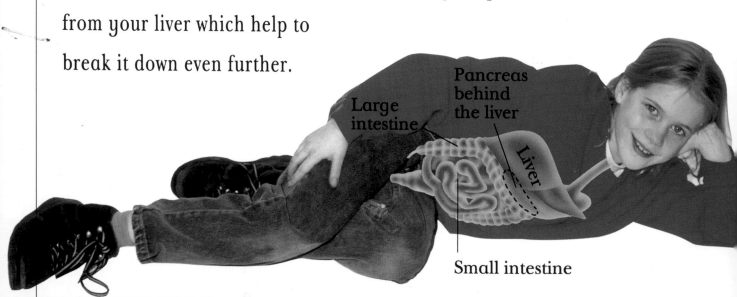

Large intestine

Pancreas behind the liver

Liver

Small intestine

It is then squeezed on through your intestine, becoming more and more watery as it goes.

As the almost-liquid food reaches the end of your small intestine, nutrients pass through its walls into your blood. The walls are lined with thousands of tiny "fingers," called villi, to help absorb the nutrients more quickly.

Your blood carries most of the nutrients to your liver. Undigested food then travels to your large intestine.

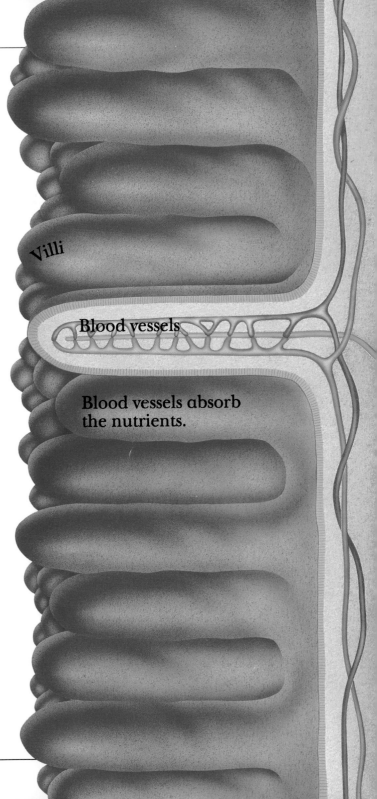

Villi

Blood vessels

Blood vessels absorb the nutrients.

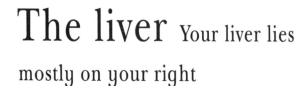

The liver

Your liver lies mostly on your right side, protected by your lower ribs. It weighs between two and four pounds. That's about the same weight as your brain.

Before any food can be used by your body, it has to be cleaned and prepared by your liver. Your liver filters the nutrients and blood to take out any leftover waste. It turns some of the waste into bile which travels through the bile ducts and out of the liver.

Liver

Gall bladder

Liver

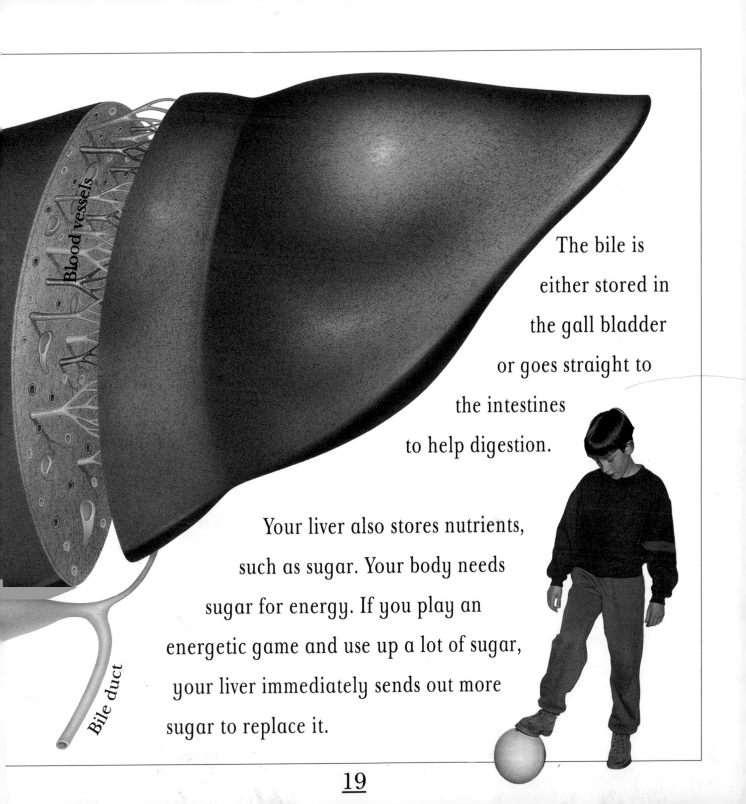

Blood vessels

Bile duct

The bile is either stored in the gall bladder or goes straight to the intestines to help digestion.

Your liver also stores nutrients, such as sugar. Your body needs sugar for energy. If you play an energetic game and use up a lot of sugar, your liver immediately sends out more sugar to replace it.

The large intestine

Your large intestine carries undigested food and water from your small intestine to your rectum.

Your large intestine is wider than your small intestine, but only half as long. It takes up to 24 hours for the contents to complete the journey from beginning to end.

As food and water travel along, a lot of water is sucked through the wall of your large intestine into your blood. Then only waste food is left. Slowly it gets harder. By the time it reaches your rectum, it is quite solid. This solid waste, called feces, is stored in your rectum until you are ready to push it out through your anus when you go to the bathroom.

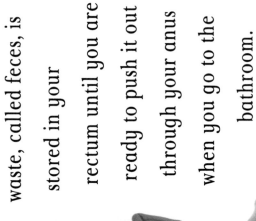

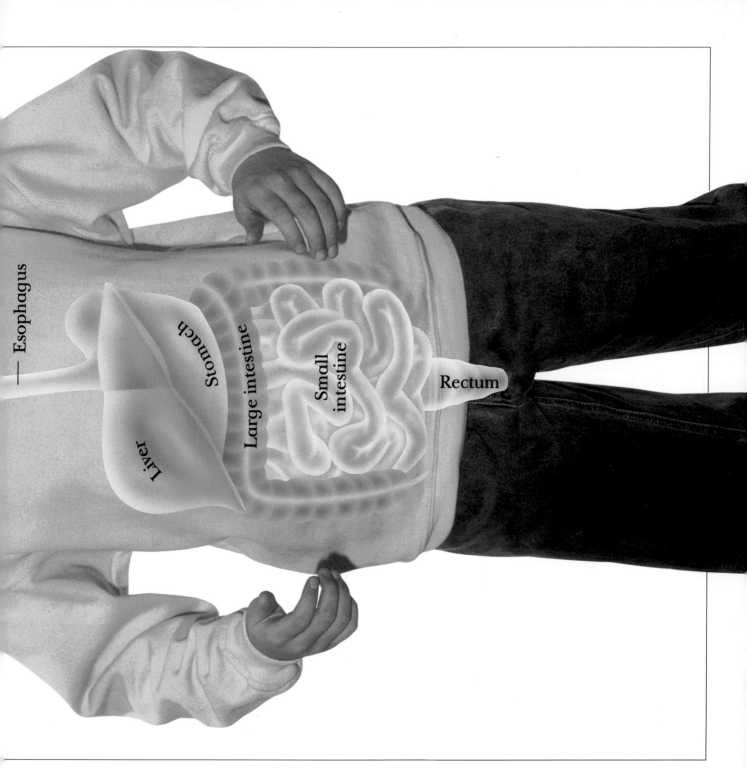

Esophagus

Liver

Stomach

Large intestine

Small intestine

Rectum

Energy

Most of the food you eat is turned into energy. Some people need more energy – and more food – than others. Babies and young children need less food than grown-ups; but as you grow into your teens you will need more.

By the time you reach your mid-teens, you will probably eat as much as your parents. Tall, well-built people need more food than shorter, thinner people. Men usually need more food than women. If you eat more food than you need it is stored as fat inside your body.

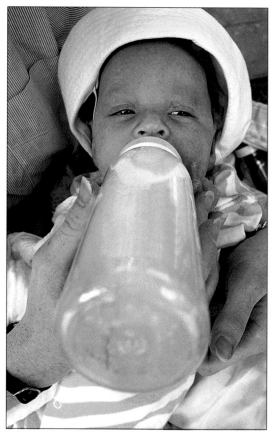

You use energy all the time. Even when you are asleep, your body is using energy to keep warm and make your heart beat. The more active you are, the more energy you use. Which of the activities shown in these pictures do you think uses up most energy? Which uses the least? Put them in order. The answers are at the bottom of the page. Look in a mirror to see if you are right.

Swimming

Watching television

Cycling

Swimming uses the most energy, followed by cycling. Watching television uses the least.

Healthy eating

Nutrients are found in food. There are five main types: proteins, carbohydrates, fats, vitamins, and minerals.

Nutrients are absorbed from the food you eat by your body. To stay healthy, you should eat the right amount of each type of nutrient every day. Each type has one or more special jobs to do in your body.

Proteins help you to grow strong and healthy. The body cannot store them so it is important to eat some food containing proteins every day. They are found in eggs, milk, cheese, fish, meat, beans, and nuts.

Bread

Potatoes

Nuts

Meat

Carbohydrates give you energy. They are found mainly in sugar, bread, and potatoes. If you eat more carbohydrates than you need over a long time, your body stores them as fat. Too much fat is unhealthy because it makes your heart work extra hard to pump blood around your body.

Cocoa

Butter

Oil

Milk

Chocolate

Eggs

Cheese

Milk

Fish

Fats are needed for growth and energy. They are found in milk, oil, butter, chocolate, and cocoa. About a third of your energy comes from the fats you eat.

You need small amounts of about twelve vitamins to keep your body working well. Most vitamins are found in several different foods. Vitamin C is present only in fresh fruits and vegetables – especially oranges. Vitamin C is important for healthy skin and bones. It also helps wounds to heal.

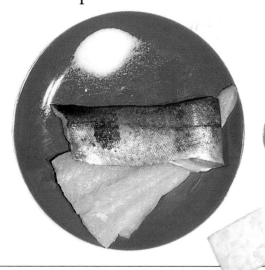

Minerals are needed only in small amounts. Calcium, in milk and cheese, helps to build healthy bones. Iodine, in fish, is important for growth.

Water

You should drink plenty of water every day. You lose up to one-and-a-half quarts (two and a quarter liters) of water each day when you breathe out, sweat, and go to the bathroom. You replace the water by eating and drinking. Half of all food is made up of water.

Ask your friends what they most like to eat. Make a chart to show everyone's favorite food. Which food do people like the best? Now plan a healthy lunch. Compare it with your favorite meal. Which is better for you?

Foods
Beans
Hamburger
Apple
Cheese
Pasta
Chocolate
Fish
Eggs

Number of people

Did you know?

... that by the age of 70, you will have eaten more than 66,000 pounds (30,000 kilograms) of food? That's the weight of six elephants.

... that although you could live for up to three weeks without food, you would die in just three days without water?

... that your body has as much calcium as 340 sticks of chalk?

... that nearly three-quarters of your body is made up of water?

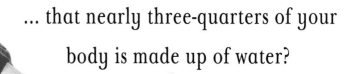

... that the human stomach can hold up to two quarts of food and water?

Compare this with a big dog – almost three quarts; a pig – between one and three gallons; a horse – between three and six gallons; a cow – 40 gallons.

... that every day you produce about one half-gallon of saliva?

Index

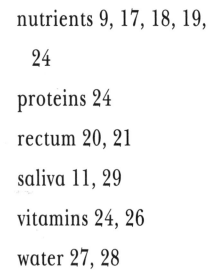
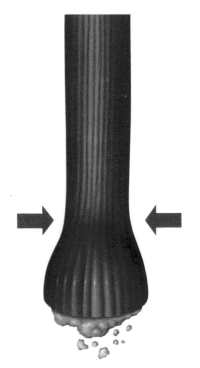
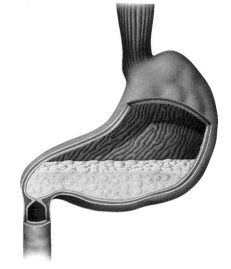